The

Art

of

the

Butterfly

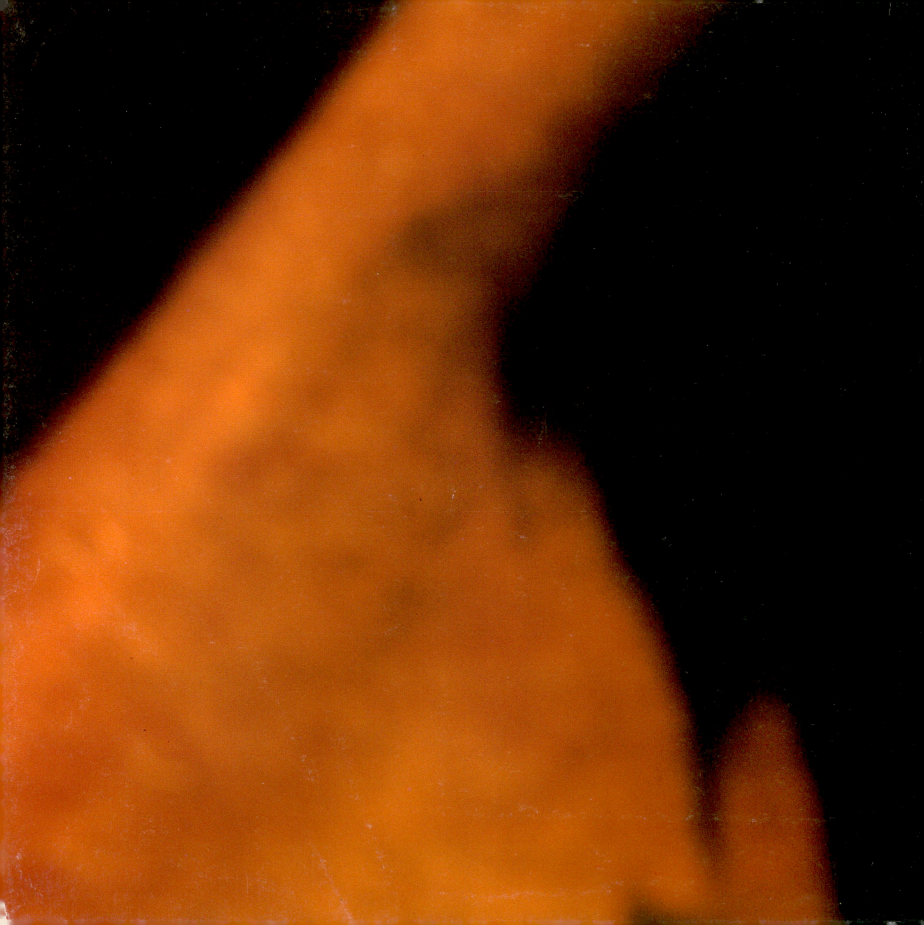

"Few things indeed have I known in the way of emotion or appetite,

ambition or achievement, that could surpass in richness and strength

the excitement of entomological exploration."

—Vladimir Nabokov
Speak, Memory

Butterflies and moths from the World Insectarium

and Butterfly Park, Singapore

The

Art

of

the

Butterfly

Ed Marquand

photographs by Michael Burns

with an afterword by Robert Michael Pyle

Chronicle Books

San Francisco

Edited, designed, and produced for Chronicle Books by Marquand Books, Inc., Seattle

Typeset by The Type Gallery, Inc., Seattle
Printed and bound in Japan by Toppan Printing Co., Ltd.
Background photography by Ed Marquand

Library of Congress Cataloging-in-Publication Data
Marquand, Ed.
The art of the butterfly / Ed Marquand: with an afterword by
Robert Michael Pyle; photographs by Michael Burns.
p.   cm.
Includes index.
ISBN 0-87701-792-1. — ISBN 0-87701-784-0 (pbk.)
1. Butterflies — Catalogs and collections. 2. Butterflies —
Catalogs and collections — Asia, Southeastern. I. Title.
QL545.2.M37   1990
595.78′9′0745957 — dc20   90-1979

Distributed in Canada by Raincoast Books
112 East 3rd Avenue, Vancouver, B.C. V5T1C8

1   3   5   7   9   10   8   6   4   2

Chronicle Books
275 Fifth Street
San Francisco, California 94103

Contents

Asia and Australia

PAPILIONIDAE
Trogonoptera trojana trojana
Palawan Island, Philippines

PAPILIONIDAE
Trogonoptera brookiana albescens
Malay Peninsula

PAPILIONIDAE
Trogonoptera brookiana albescens
Malay Peninsula

Neocheritra gertrudes
Mindanao Island, Philippines

Tajuria berensis
Malay Peninsula

Arhopala trogon
Singapore

Neomyrina nivea
Malay Peninsula

Sithon nedymond
Malay Peninsula

Drupadia ravindra
Malay Peninsula

Dacalana aristarchus
Mindanao Island, Philippines

LYCAENIDAE

5

LYCAENIDAE

Drina mavortia
Mindanao Island, Philippines

Rapala domitia
Malay Peninsula

Eliotia mioae
Mindanao Island, Philippines

Arhopala anthelus
Malay Peninsula

⑥

LYCAENIDAE

Arhopala staudingeri
Mindanao Island, Philippines

Cheritra freja
Malay Peninsula

Eliotia mioae
Mindanao Island, Philippines

PAPILIONIDAE
Ornithoptera alexandrae alexandrae
(male)
Papua New Guinea

7

PAPILIONIDAE
Ornithoptera alexandrae alexandrae
(female)
Papua New Guinea

PAPILIONIDAE
Ornithoptera goliath joiceyi
Irian Jaya, Indonesia

PAPILIONIDAE
Ornithoptera paradisea paradisea
Irian Jaya, Indonesia, and Papua New Guinea

10

PAPILIONIDAE

Agehana elwesi elwesi
South and West China

Papilio memnon agenor
Malay Peninsula

12

PAPILIONIDAE
Losaria coon doubledai
Malay Peninsula;
Java and Sumatra, Indonesia

13

PAPILIONIDAE

Papilio hoppo hoppo
Taiwan

Papilio chikae chikae
North Luzon Island, Philippines

PAPILIONIDAE
Papilio blumei blumei
South Celebes Islands, Indonesia

15

PAPILIONIDAE

Papilio ulysses
Seram Island, Indonesia

Papilio ulysses joesa
Australia

Papilio pericles pericles
Timor and Tanimbar Islands, Indonesia

16

PAPILIONIDAE

Papilio neumoegeni neumoegeni
Sumba Island, Indonesia

PAPILIONIDAE
Troides prattorum prattorum
Buru Islands, Indonesia

PAPILIONIDAE
Troides hypolitus hypolitus
Celebes, Ambon, Seram, and Buru Islands, Indonesia

PAPILIONIDAE
Troides helena cerber
(Gynandromorph)
Malay Peninsula

PAPILIONIDAE

Atorophaneura semperi aphthonia
(male)
Mindanao Island, Philippines

Atorophaneura semperi aphthonia
(female)
Mindanao Island, Philippines

PAPILIONIDAE
Papilio ascalaphus ascalaphus
Celebes Islands, Indonesia

AMATHUSIDAE
Enispe euthymius
Malay Peninsula

NYMPHALIDAE
Prothoe calydonia calydonia
Malay Peninsula

23

Nymphalidae
Yoma sabina
Celebes Islands, Indonesia

Kallima paralekta amplirufa
Malay Peninsula

NYMPHALIDAE

Kallima paralekta paralekta
Java, Indonesia

Kallima inachus formosana
(underside)
Taiwan

PAPILIONIDAE
Graphium decolor
Palawan Island, Philippines

PIERIDAE
Delias apoensis apoensis
Mindanao Island, Philippines

NYMPHALIDAE

Euthalia adonia adonia
Java, Indonesia

Euthalia amanda amanda
Celebes Islands, Indonesia

27

Danaidae

Euploea configurata configurata
Celebes Islands, Indonesia

Euploea blossomae
Luzon Island, Philippines

DANAIDAE
Parantica dannatti dannatti
Mindanao Island, Philippines

DANAIDAE
Idea blanchardii marosiana
South Celebes Islands, Indonesia

Idea lynceus lynceus
Malay Peninsula;
Java, Sumatra, and Borneo, Indonesia

Idea idea idea
Ambon and Seram Islands, Indonesia

30

DANAIDAE

Cethosia hypsea hypsea
Malay Peninsula

NYMPHALIDAE

Cethosia biblis perakana
Malay Peninsula

PAPILIONIDAE
Bhutanitis lidderdalei
North Thailand

NYMPHALIDAE

Polyura dehaani sultan
Sumatra, Indonesia

Polyura cognata cognata
Celebes Islands, Indonesia

PIERIDAE
Hebomoia glaucippe aturia
Malay Peninsula

NYMPHALIDAE
Polyura jalysus jalysus
Malay Peninsula

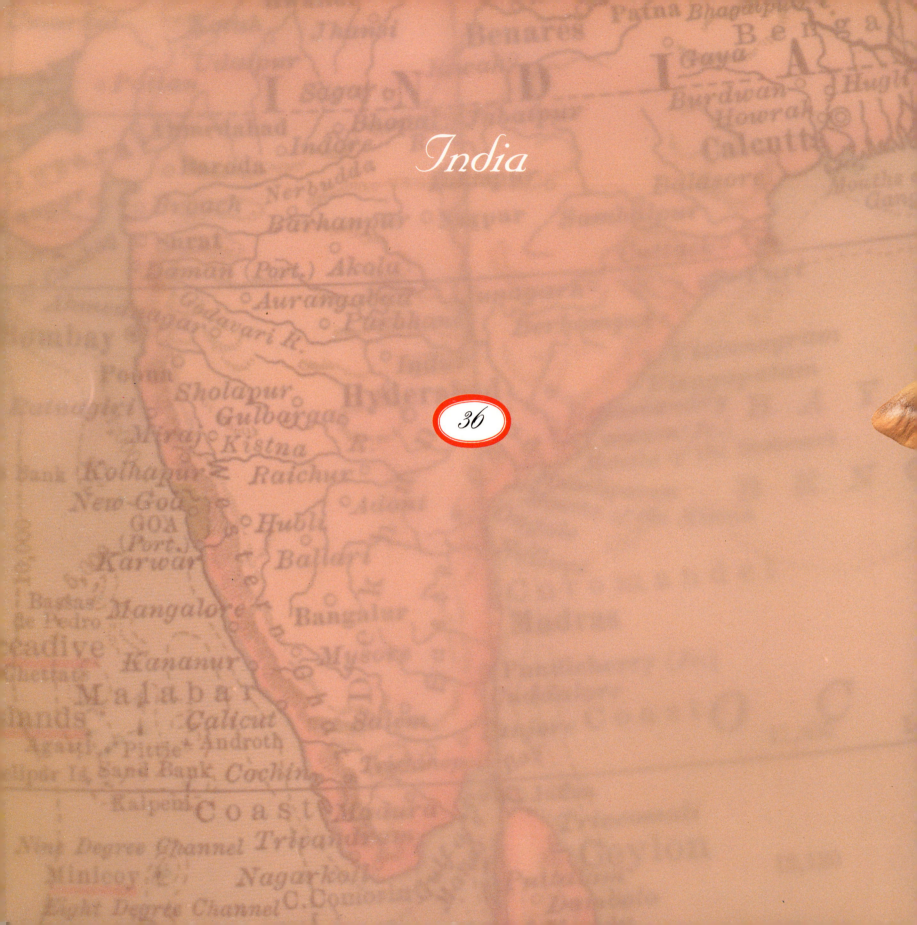

SATURNIIDAE (moth)
Antheraea jana
India to Southeast Asia

SPHINGIDAE (moth)
Cherontia lachesis
India to Southeast Asia

Teinopalpus imperialis imperialis
(female)
North India

38

NYMPHALIDAE

Teinopalpus imperialis imperialis
(male)
North India

PAPILIONIDAE
Papilio polymnestor parinda
Sri Lanka

40

PAPILIONIDAE
Byasa polyeuctes letincius
North India, Nepal, and Kashmir

South America

Chorinea faunus
South America

Ancyluris meliboeus
Amazon to Peru

NEMEOBIIDAE

ITHOMIIDAE
Thyridia psidii
Peru and Brazil

HELICONIDAE
Philaethria dido
Central America to South Brazil

43

NEMEOBIIDAE

Caligo eurilochus
Peru

Caligo placidianus
Peru

MORPHIDAE
Morpho menelaus
Guianas to Bolivia

MORPHIDAE

Morpho didius
Peru and Bolivia

Morpho sulkouskyi
Brazil

NYMPHALIDAE
Callicore pastazza
Peru

NEMEOBIIDAE
Lyropteryx apollonia
Ecuador to Bolivia and Brazil

NYMPHALIDAE
Callicore aegina
Peru

NYMPHALIDAE
Perisama vaninka
Peru

NYMPHALIDAE
Callicore hesperis
South America

NYMPHALIDAE
Cymothoe rheinoldi
Africa

PAPILIONIDAE
Papilio demodocus
Africa (except North)

PAPILIONIDAE
Papilio ophidicephalus
East Africa to South Africa

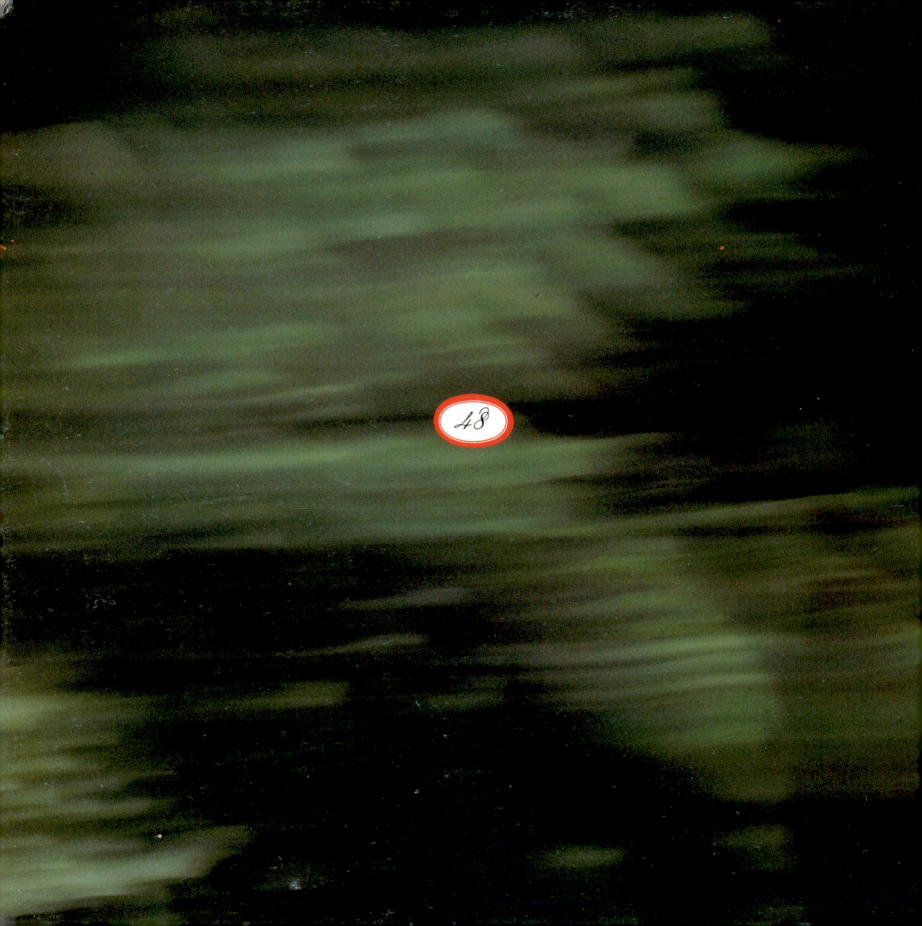

URANIIDAE (moth)
Chrysiridia madagascariensis
Madagascar

PAPILIONIDAE
Dururya antimachus
Cameroon

NYMPHALIDAE

Charaxes andoronodorus
Madagascar

Hypolymnas dexithea
Madagascar

"Through the smells of the bog, I caught the subtle perfume of butterfly wings on my fingers, a perfume which varies with the species — vanilla, or lemon, or musk, or a musty, sweetish odor difficult to define. Still unsated, I pressed forward . . . .

"I confess I do not believe in time. I like to fold my magic carpet, after use, in such a way as to superimpose one part of the pattern upon another. Let visitors trip. And the highest enjoyment of timelessness — in a landscape selected at random — is when I stand among rare butterflies and their food plants. This is ecstasy, and behind the ecstasy is something else, which is hard to explain. It is like a momentary vacuum into which rushes all that I love. A sense of oneness with sun and stone. A thrill of gratitude to whom it may concern — to the contrapuntal genius of human fate or to tender ghosts humoring a lucky mortal."

— Vladimir Nabokov
Speak, Memory

Afterword

Our government Land Cruiser came to a stop in the shade of a tropical palm, beside a sign that read, simply, Oomsis. I stepped out into the equatorial heat. I'd already seen enough of Papua New Guinea to know that the forest around me would be teeming with life. But when my eyes adjusted to the brilliant sunshine, I beheld a spectacle unlike any I'd ever imagined. A tall acacia tree, spangled with yellow blossoms, served as center of the universe to a whirling mass of brilliant butterflies.

Green birdwings, the size of dinner plates, circled the nectar banquet. Black-and-white citrus swallowtails flapped everywhere. A crimson-spotted species called Polydorus flitted through the dappled light on the forest edge. Big purple hairstreaks zipped among the shrubbery. It was hard to keep my eyes on any one sight. Then I focused on the acacia, and on the great Ulysses swallowtails taking nourishment there: expansive creatures, four inches across their stunning wings, black velvet edges framing metallic sky-blue centers. I was transported by the sheer beauty of tropical butterflies.

Since then, I have been fortunate to witness many grand butterfly spectacles. I have walked among the massed monarchs of Mexico in their cinnamon millions, watched iridescent blue morphos sail out across the Caribbean in Costa Rica, and spotted African blue pansies and crimson-tips amid the jungle and the veldt.

Yet, whenever I think of exotic insects, Oomsis comes to mind, and that first memorable immersion in the extraordinary colors and diversity of the butterflies of the tropics. I also think of their fate, as we continue to disrupt the unimaginably complex systems of rain forests and other ecosystems of the tropic realm.

Butterflies and moths, known together as Lepidoptera, are four-winged insects painted by millions of tiny scales that either reflect or diffract light. They reach their greatest variety in the tropics, following the ecological principle that life becomes more diverse the nearer one approaches the equator. The Arctic and Antarctic regions have many individual organisms (mosquitoes and caribou, penguins and seals) but far fewer species than the equatorial climes. The warmth and moisture of the tropics encourage great diversification of plant and animal life. This is why damage to tropical rain forests affects many more kinds of life than alterations elsewhere.

While butterflies are beautiful wherever they occur, it stands to reason that the rich butterfly fauna of the tropics would contain more brilliant and spectacular types than the temperate array. And so it does. The palette presented by tropical butterfly wings is colorful almost beyond comprehension. For this reason, collectors and museums have long coveted representatives of these species for their cabinets. Hunters with butterfly nets make obvious targets for blame when butterfly populations fall. Consequently, when Rajah Brooke's birdwing, an emerald-and-jet giant, diminished in Malaysia, the government prohibited collecting. Other countries have followed suit.

Collecting restrictions, however, have done little to save wild butterflies. It turns out that most butterflies, like other insects, are extremely difficult to over-collect because of their terrific ability to reproduce. Furthermore, butterfly collections have always served to raise public interest in these creatures and their requirements. In fact, several tropical nations have turned to butterfly farming in order to raise needed cash in villages while enhancing the numbers of local butterflies in the wild. My purpose for going to Oomsis was to assist in the development of an insect farming and conservation program for Papua New Guinea. Now the neighboring country of Irian Jaya (Indonesian New Guinea) and several other butterfly-rich countries are ranching desirable species. This takes pressure off the wild populations while providing stock for butterfly houses around the world, specimens for collectors, and an income for villagers. Perhaps most important, ranching gives an incentive for protecting nearby butterfly habitats.

Truly it is the destruction of their habitats that endangers many tropical butterflies, rather than collecting. Butterflies in the tropics occupy specialized habitats where their caterpillars feed only on certain kinds of plants. Some species are adapted for savannah grasslands, threatened by drought and overgrazing by domestic livestock. Others dwell in coastal and interior swamps, in jeopardy from wetland drainage and sea-level changes due to global warming.

By far the greatest number of tropical butterflies and moths lives in forest environments—the so-called rain forests, or tropical moist forests, of which we hear so much these days. And for good reason. Deforestation due to clearance for short-term agriculture, reservoirs and power projects, hardwood logging and pulp extraction, and the sheer pressure of expanding populations bring about the destruction of thousands of acres of rain forest habitat daily. The situation is urgent. The loss of biological diversity puts long-term evolutionary prospects at risk, while the opening of the forest canopy exacerbates the greenhouse effect by reducing much of the earth's ability to process carbon dioxide. But many people are working in good faith to arrest these losses, and there is some reason to hope that we might recognize and respect the enormous value of the tropical forest in time to save it.

We could do worse than to watch tropical butterflies as we work to save the tropics, either in nature or through the lens of the camera and the reports of scientists in the field. For one thing, butterflies serve as elegant and valuable indicators of habitat health. Conspicuous and sensitive, they drop out of ecosystems when things go wrong with the flora, the microclimate, and other elements of the system. It is vital that we catalog the butterfly and other insect faunas of these special places, and continue to monitor them, in order to better recognize the early signs of ecosystem failure. Here is where the butterfly collector can perform real service to conservation.

For another, beautiful butterflies have a way of refueling the spirit in a way I have seldom found elsewhere—as they did for me that day in New Guinea, at the forest of Oomsis. You needn't be a lepidopterist with a net to appreciate this. Simply beholding the beauty of butterflies, undistracted—in person, or in a book such as this—you will find yourself delighted, refreshed, and emboldened to take part in the great human adventure of discovering, loving, and caring for our rich natural world.

—Robert Michael Pyle

Butterfly and Rain Forest Conservation

The primary organization working for the conservation of rare butterflies and the habitats of all beneficial invertebrates is The Xerces Society. Founded in 1971 and named for the extinct Xerces blue butterfly (extirpated on the San Francisco Peninsula about 1941), the Society has an international membership devoted to education about the positive roles of nonpest insects and the conservation of invertebrate habitats in both the temperate and tropical worlds. The Society publishes the journal *Atala* and the magazine *Wings* and conducts annual butterfly counts in many locations. Information may be obtained by writing to The Xerces Society, 10 SW Ash Street, Portland, Oregon, 97204.

Many organizations are seeking solutions to tropical rain forest conservation problems. The following groups can provide details on how you can help: Rainforest Action Network, 300 Broadway, Suite 28, San Francisco, California, 94133; World Wildlife Fund, 1250 24th Street NW, Washington, D.C., 20037; and Conservation International, 1015 18th Street NW, Suite 1002, Washington, D.C., 20036.

World Insectarium and Butterfly Park

The tropical butterflies and moths that make up this volume were selected from the collection of the World Insectarium and Butterfly Park on Sentosa Island, Singapore. Founded in 1983, this delightful facility houses over three thousand mounted specimens and features approximately sixty live species in a large outdoor conservatory where visitors can closely observe butterflies in all stages of development and activity.

Tropical butterflies and insects from Southeast Asia make up 80 percent of the World Insectarium collection, which also includes spectacular examples from South America, Africa, and the rest of Asia.

With butterfly breeding farms and insectariums in Penang and Sarawak, Malaysia, the World Insectarium conducts valuable research and assists scholars and scientists from around the world in their studies of the insects of Southeast Asia and of tropical rain forests.

Acknowledgments

The author gratefully acknowledges the assistance and cooperation of the World Insectarium and Butterfly Park, Sentosa, Singapore. Managing partner Chiang Sing Jeong, his former assistant, Irene Ee, and a capable staff made this project a distinct pleasure. Hiromi Detani provided critical identifications, and Leonard Yeo offered valuable leads in getting the project underway.

Thanks must also go to Bernie Veldhoen, who encouraged me to visit Sentosa Island in the first place, to John Stevenson and Michele Clise for their perceptive suggestions, and to Barbara Davis for leading me to Robert Michael Pyle.

56

Index

The numbers below refer to spread numbers, which are found on
each set of facing pages within a red oval.